THE
WORRY

MW01171759

"OVERCOMING WORRY AND FEAR **FOREVER**"

WRITTEN

BY

KEVIN WRIGHT

THE WAR ON WORRY

THE WAR ON WORRY

THE WAR ON WORRY

THE WAR ON WORRY

"OVERCOMING WORRY AND FEAR FOREVER"

WRITTEN BY KEVIN WRIGHT

ALL SCRIPTURE TAKEN FROM THE KING JAMES VERSION UNLESS OTHERWISE INDICATED.

SCRIPTURE QUOTATIONS MARKED AMP ARE TAKEN FROM AMPLIFIED BIBLE, COPYRIGHT © 2015 BY THE LOCKMAN FOUNDATION, LA HABRA, CA 90631. ALL RIGHTS RESERVED.

SCRIPTURE QUOTATIONS MARKED AMPC ARE TAKEN FROM AMPLIFIED BIBLE, CLASSIC EDITION, COPYRIGHT © 1954, 1958, 1962, 1964, 1965, 1987 BY THE LOCKMAN FOUNDATION.

SCRIPTURE QUOTATIONS MARKED MSG ARE TAKEN FROM THE MESSAGE, COPYRIGHT © 1993, 2002, 2018 BY EUGENE H. PETERSON.

SCRIPTURE QUOTATIONS MARKED NKJV ARE TAKEN FROM SCRIPTURE TAKEN FROM THE NEW KING JAMES VERSION®, COPYRIGHT © 1982 BY THOMAS NELSON. USED BY PERMISSION. ALL RIGHTS RESERVED.

SCRIPTURE QUOTATIONS MARKED PHILLIPS ARE TAKEN FROM THE NEW TESTAMENT IN MODERN ENGLISH BY J.B. PHILLIPS, COPYRIGHT © 1960, 1972 J. B. PHILLIPS. ADMINISTERED BY THE ARCHBISHOPS' COUNCIL OF THE CHURCH OF ENGLAND. USED BY PERMISSION.

SCRIPTURE QUOTATIONS MARKED TLB ARE TAKEN FROM THE LIVING BIBLE, COPYRIGHT © 1971 BY TYNDALE HOUSE FOUNDATION. USED BY PERMISSION OF TYNDALE HOUSE PUBLISHERS INC., CAROL STREAM, ILLINOIS 60188. ALL RIGHTS RESERVED.

FIRST EDITION

ISBN: 979-8-218-53985-6

CONTENTS

INTRODUCTION

We were just little kids growing up in a small town in Pulaski, Tennessee. My brother Brian and I spent most of our time outdoors. Our greatest passion for the outdoors was deer hunting. I was around ten years old, and Brian would take me on deer hunts in the woods next to our house. I remember my mom always worrying about us boys as we walked off in the dark before the sun came up into the dark forest.

Back then, we didn't have cell phones to use if there was an emergency. We had curfews to be home at whatever time mom told us. When we would break those curfews, and we did all the time, my mom would be waiting on us worried and upset. Her words would always be, "You had me worried sick over you boys." Then, we would get the belt!

Now, back then my mom didn't know how to pray the Word and use her faith like she does now. She would literally worry until we got back home. Our mom would imagine some of the worst things in her mind while she would wait for us to get back home from hunting. I'm sure she worried that we got lost or accidentally shot. I think it's crazy how the worst thoughts can come to us when we worry about something. I remember my mom raising us by herself, and I'm sure she also worried about money, worried about the future, worried about how wild her boys were, and where they would end up in life.

Mom was a worrier. She always had a very strong love for her boys and that was the excuse for why she worried so much. I believe mom passed down her worry habits to us. As we got older, we began to worry just like her. Now that we are adults, I realize we can inherit worry and fear just like some people have certain diseases that run through their families. It can be passed down from generation to generation until someone stops the worry and fear in its tracks. Worry declares an all-out WAR on our minds and can really do damage if we let it. That's why I'm writing this book so you can stop worry before it stops you!

I found this out about worry — worry wants to be your best friend. If worry could hang out with you 100% of the time, it would. Why? Because there is always something to worry about. Worry about your bills, worry about your job, worry about your kids, worry about money. Worry is always in the reach of every person. If Satan can get you to worry all the time, he will keep you living in fear and rob you of your peace for the rest of your life. When your joy and peace are gone, here comes worry's relatives which are anxiety, depression and discouragement.

Not all families come from a heritage of faith. Some have to start the heritage! When I was a kid, I didn't know how to live and walk by faith. I wasn't raised hearing the Word of God. We were taught to pray, but as my mom said to me one day, we didn't have a personal relationship with Jesus. We didn't even know that we could. As kids, we didn't know how to resist fear, recognize it as an enemy, and not yield to it!

As a kid, I remember struggling with fear all the time. I was afraid of the dark. I was afraid of what was in my closet. My brother and I had two double beds in our bedroom across from each other. One night, I woke up and in between our beds, on the floor was a sleeping bag that I thought was a hippopotamus. I tried to whisper to my brother that this large animal had made it into our bedroom somehow, but Brian was sound asleep. So, I leaped from my bed onto my brother's bed to escape the dangerous hippo. I'm sure he thought a hippo landed on *him*. It's pretty amazing how fear can make you see things that don't even exist.

As an adult, I still experience fear and worry in the same ways that I did as a kid. Fear and worry still try to paint the worst pictures in our minds. I remember my brother taking me deer hunting and

leaving me in the deer stand to hunt alone
for the first time when I was ten years old.
As he walked off, the darkness of the woods
began to speak. I started looking around as
I sat in that deer stand, and I saw a limb
close to me hanging from a tree. I didn't
think it was a limb though. I thought it was
a man hanging from a tree by a rope. I
screamed as loud as I could to get my
brother back to the stand. My brother
came running to my tree stand thinking I
was in danger. I told him there was a man
hanging in the tree. He took out his
flashlight and shined it on the hanging tree
limb. I can see him right now shaking his
head, looking at me, and maybe, he was
tempted to hang me on a limb!

If you allow fear and its voice into
your life, it can make you believe you are
going to die early. It can make you believe
that you are a failure. It can make you
believe that the plane you're on is going to
crash in the middle of the ocean. It can
make you believe that the wart on your
thumb is cancer. There are all kinds of fears
in this world. There are people who are
afraid of butterflies. There are people who

are afraid of peanut butter sticking to the roof of their mouths, fear of not having their phones, fear about where their next meal is going to come from, fear of death, fear of water, fear of bathing, and fear of making decisions. I'm telling you that I could do page after page of fears or what we call phobias.

We live in a worry and fear driven world. That's why I'm writing this book to help teach you how to win the war on worry. I have outlined in this book how God showed me how to get free from fear and worry. No matter what worry or fear you may be facing, God has the antidote that can take care of it. It's called the Word of God, and He can and will chase fear out of your life forever.

When I was nineteen, I gave my life to Jesus, and for the first time, I realized the authority I had in Christ. I don't have to live in worry and fear anymore. I found out that God loves me, and if God loves me, then He is going to take care of every problem I face in life. My faith in the love of God was the beginning of defeating worry and fear.

Although worry and fear will never be far from your reach, they are NOT our go-to anymore when we face difficulty! Faith in the love of God is our go-to. Get ready, as we dive into the scripture and discover our freedom and authority over fear and worry and how to win the war on worry forever.

CHAPTER 1

THE DANGERS OF WORRY

I believe the first step in winning the war on worry is to understand what worry really means. If you think about the word *worry*, it seems so innocent and harmless, but as you read the definition below, you will see this little word called *worry* is very dangerous.

DEFINITION OF WORRY

In the *Merriam Webster dictionary* the meaning of the word *worry* means: "to afflict with mental distress or agitation: make anxious: to harass by tearing, biting, or snapping especially at the throat: to shake or pull at with the teeth: to touch or disturb something repeatedly: to change the position of or adjust by repeated pushing or hauling: to assail with rough or aggressive attack or treatment: TORMENT: to subject to persistent or nagging attention or effort: CHOKE, STRANGLE."

Worry, according to this definition, is designed to afflict, agitate and cause mental distress. Worry has a huge role in making a person feel anxious and will harass a person, like a dog biting its prey at the throat! Worry will try to touch and attack your thought life repeatedly until it torments you and ultimately chokes the life out of you. That's a scary picture of worry.

THE PURPOSE OF WORRY

If worry is designed to choke or strangle, what is worry choking or strangling in your life? Worry will choke your joy and keep you from smiling. It can choke your physical and mental health. Worry can rob you of your sleep. Worry can zap your energy right out of your life and ultimately lead to discouragement and depression.

Excessive worrying and high anxiety are known to lead to depression and even suicidal thoughts. The biggest thing worry wants to choke out of your life is the Word of God. The Bible tells us that worry is designed to do just that — choke the Word right out of our hearts.

Mark 4:18-19 (AMP) says, "And others are the ones on whom seed was sown among the thorns; these are the ones who have heard the word, but the

worries *and* cares of the world [the distractions of this age with its worldly pleasures], and the deceitfulness [and the false security or glamour] of wealth [or fame], and the passionate desires for all the other things creep in and choke out the word, and it becomes unfruitful."

Here, we see in Scripture that worries and the cares of this world have the ability to creep in and choke the Word of God in our hearts. The purpose of worry is to choke the life right out of you. If worry chokes the Word, then worry will choke out your faith. The Scripture says that the worry and the cares of the world creep in and choke the Word. But how? How can worry have any power over the Word of God? It's because we have allowed worry to dominate our thinking to the point we are no longer in faith but in fear. Whatever we pay attention to is what we feed, so to speak. If fear comes, and we pay attention to fear, then we begin to feed fear. Fear will begin to grow more and more as we give it attention. If we feed our faith and starve our fears, our faith will grow more and more. There is a real grappling match happening between faith and fear.

This is how I allowed the enemy to use worry to choke the Word of God out of my heart. I have so many memories of giving into worry and fear and falling right into the devil's discouragement. I spent many sleepless nights tossing and turning and worrying. I went from happy and full of joy one day to living in fear and having no peace the next day. We have all probably tried to get peace by going on vacations and spending thousands of dollars to travel and clear our minds. I remember sitting on the most beautiful tropical island on vacation, listening to the waves crash on the beach, sitting there under a palm tree, but worried about some things going on in my life. I was letting the enemy steal my peace and my joy and my vacation in the middle of paradise. Paradise won't cure worry on the inside of you. The Word of God can get rid of worry, and you can have paradise happening on the inside and the outside.

For over fourteen years I have trained in jiu-jitsu, and over those years, I have learned to grapple with opponents and how to submit them. Submit means you force your opponent to give up or tap out. I'm going to teach you how to tap out fear with your faith. You have to win the grappling match and submit worry so worry never has a chance to tap you out or make you quit!

THE AUTHOR OF WORRY AND FEAR

Worry has always been a thief that weakens and attacks your faith! Worry constantly lies against the truth and directly contradicts the Word of God. Why do worry and fear contradict the Word? The answer is that God is not the author of fear and has no fear or worry to give us.

In 2 Timothy 1:7 it says, "For God hath not given us the spirit of fear; but of power, and of love, and of a sound mind."

If God didn't give us fear, then who is behind fear? Satan is behind fear, and he needs us to have fear so he can have access in our lives. Fear is the open door for the spirit of fear to come into our lives. If the enemy can get you and I in fear, then he will steal our peace and our joy by getting us to doubt the truth. Satan has used fear from the very beginning of the creation of man. We see how the devil used fear to tempt Adam and Eve in the garden.

> **Now the serpent was more subtil than any beast of the field which the LORD God had made. And he said unto the woman, Yea, hath God said, Ye shall not eat of every tree of the garden?**
>
> **And the woman said unto the serpent, We may eat of the fruit of the trees of the garden:**
>
> **But of the fruit of the tree which is in the midst of the garden, God hath said, Ye shall not eat of it, neither shall ye touch it, lest ye die.**
>
> **And the serpent said unto the woman, Ye shall not surely die:**

For God doth know that in the day ye eat thereof, then your eyes shall be opened, and ye shall be as gods, knowing good and evil.

And when the woman saw that the tree was good for food, and that it was pleasant to the eyes, and a tree to be desired to make one wise, she took of the fruit thereof, and did eat, and gave also unto her husband with her; and he did eat.

And the eyes of them both were opened, and they knew that they were naked; and they sewed fig leaves together, and made themselves aprons.

And they heard the voice of the LORD God walking in the garden in the cool of the day: and Adam and his wife hid themselves from the presence of the LORD God amongst the trees of the garden (Genesis 3:1-8).

When Satan was tempting Eve, he had to make her to think God didn't give her everything she needed in the garden. He used fear to make her feel incomplete. I believe it was fear that opened the door to the fall of man in the garden. Satan used fear to make Eve feel that she didn't know good from evil. She felt for the first time she didn't have everything she needed from God. Satan made the forbidden tree look attractive through fear! Guess what? Satan is still up to the same tactics as he was in the garden. Look at what happened after Adam and Eve sinned.

And they heard the voice of the LORD God walking in the garden in the cool of the day: and Adam and his wife hid themselves from the presence of the LORD God amongst the trees of the garden.

And the LORD God called unto Adam, and said unto him, Where art thou?

And he said, I heard thy voice in the garden, and I was afraid, because I was naked; and I hid myself.

And he said, Who told thee that thou wast naked? Hast thou eaten of the tree, whereof I commanded thee that thou shouldest not eat? (Genesis 3:8-11).

Until that moment, fear and worry were not a part of human vocabulary. Adam and Eve lived in total provision, and everything was supplied for them by God. In the garden the animals were friendly, there was an abundance of food, and they had all authority. There was no sickness or death or poverty. Every evening God would come and walk with Adam and Eve and talk to His creation. Then sin came and changed everything. Fear was born in the heart of man. Adam and Eve were no longer clothed in God's righteousness, and they knew for the first time they were naked. Naked and afraid! They were in fear and hid themselves from God. Satan found a way to enter into their beautiful world through fear to ultimately steal, kill and destroy using fear to accomplish the fall of man.

When Adam and Eve left the garden, they would experience a world full of fear for the first time. Life was drastically different now that fear had entered their lives. Their son, Cain, killed their other son, Abel. Satan used fear to make Cain jealous of Abel's offering to the Lord, so he killed Abel over an offering. We now have a glimpse of the war on worry and fear from the beginning of creation until now.

In **John 10:10 (AMP) it says, "The thief comes only in order to steal and kill and destroy. I came that they may have *and* enjoy life, and have it in abundance [to the full, till it overflows]."**

Satan is a thief and he's out to kill and destroy life. Let me tell you one of the open doors the enemy uses to steal, kill and destroy. It's fear and worry! How many people on the planet are being tormented by fear? I know I have allowed the enemy to torment me over the years. I'm so glad I know my authority now and how to stop worry and fear in its tracks. I'm so excited to share with you how I did it so you can do it too!

CHAPTER 2

DON'T TAKE THE THOUGHT

I've got some good news for all of us. We don't have to let worry and fear control our lives and our thoughts. They may be within arm's reach at any time day or night, but we have a choice in the matter of whether we allow them to control us. We are going to learn how to stop worrying by stopping the thoughts that bring worry. So, let's look at the Word of God and find out how we can stop worry and fear forever.

Matthew 6:25 says, "Therefore I say unto you, Take no thought for your life, what ye shall eat, or what ye shall drink; nor yet for your body, what ye shall put on. Is not the life more than meat, and the body than raiment?"

Take No Thought

I'm going to give you two translations of this verse so we can understand what Jesus is saying a little better. In the King James Version, Jesus says, **"Take no thought about what you may eat, what you shall drink, what you shall wear."** So, in this passage of scripture, Jesus is telling us to NOT take certain thoughts. We have a choice of whether or not we are going to take a fear or worry thought. Let's look at the Amplified version.

> **"Therefore I tell you, stop being worried *or* anxious (perpetually uneasy, distracted) about your life, as to what you will eat or what you will drink; nor about your body, as to what you will wear. Is life not more than food, and the body more than clothing?"**

Stop Worry Thinking

The Amplified translation tells us to "STOP being worried and anxious." Both translations sound like commands to me. We are commanded not to take worry or anxious thoughts. We are commanded to "STOP being worried and anxious." If Jesus was standing before you and me, face to face, and said these words, what would your response be? I can picture Jesus telling me this face to face. I see Him saying to me, "Kevin, STOP worrying and being in fear over this! Don't take any more thoughts of worry and fear! Kevin stop

22

being anxious." Jesus is saying to me face to face to stop it!

We need to know what to take into our thinking and what to NOT take into our thinking. Your mind is your mind, and it's your responsibility to allow certain thoughts or stop certain thoughts. We also determine how long certain thoughts linger in our mind. You may not like to hear this, but God is not going to take your thoughts from you. You are the CEO of your mind. You decide what gets in or what stays out. You can't keep thoughts from coming your way. I like what one preacher said about thoughts, "You can't keep birds from flying over your head, but you can keep them from nesting in your hair." A thought may enter my thought life, but I am the determining factor if it stays or goes!

S h i f t   Y o u r   F o c u s

In **Mathew 6:26-27 it says, "Behold the fowls of the air: for they sow not, neither do they reap, nor gather into**

barns; yet your heavenly Father feedeth them. Are ye not much better than they? Which of you by taking thought can add one cubit unto his stature?"

In the Living Bible it says, **"Look at the birds! They don't worry about what to eat—they don't need to sow or reap or store up food—for your heavenly Father feeds them. And you are far more valuable to him than they are."**

Jesus tells us to get our eyes off of the problem and go bird watching. Sounds kind of comical that Jesus would want us to get our eyes off of worry and fear and go bird watching. Why bird watching? The answer is: birds are not worried. They don't sow and neither do they harvest food, but God takes care of them. When I look at the birds, I don't see any starving birds.

What Jesus says about bird watching makes sense to me when I'm deer hunting. When I'm hunting and I'm watching the deer step out of the forest into the open field, I'm not thinking about anything else in my life at that moment. Well, I might be thinking about that big buck that's staging that field and about to step out, but I'm NOT worried about anything going on in my life at that moment.

Jesus loved the outdoors, and He preached outdoors. He walked everywhere outdoors. I could see Him literally pointing at some birds up in a tree and saying, "Look at the birds." Maybe we need to go on more walks outdoors and go bird watching. Watch the birds fly, watch them sing, and listen to the pretty sounds that they make. Look at those birds while you're walking and see how they are not worried. They have no food shortage. They are not running out of worms and insects to eat.

You Are so Valuable

Jesus wants us to look at the birds, and then points out that we are more valuable than the birds! We are so very valuable to God, and He wants to take good care of us. God takes care of the birds, and I've got a good feeling He's going to take care of us. He doesn't want us worried about anything just like the birds don't worry about a food shortage or where they're going to nest. I believe God is saying to us, "Stop giving the problems so much attention." Shift your focus to how the birds are taken care of by your Heavenly Father. You're more valuable than birds. Maybe it's time to stop giving these problems and worries and fears so much of your attention and so much value.

I love the song by Elevation and Maverick City — "Jireh." The lyrics of the song say:

"If he dresses the lilies with beauty and splendor
How much more will He clothe you?
If He watches over every sparrow
How much more does He love you?"

This song is such a reminder of how much your Heavenly Father loves you! He doesn't want you weighed down with worry and fear. He is a loving Father who wants to take care of every battle and problem you face.

Satan is always bombarding us with horrible thoughts! Isn't it crazy how we can take thoughts from someone who hates us (Satan) and not take thoughts from the One who loves us? The devil can't force you to think his thoughts. We have power and authority over the enemy and his tempting thoughts. He can bring a thought a thousand times, but you don't have to take the thought a thousand times. Don't take the thought! Remember, you're the CEO of your thought life.

How Do You Take a Thought?

Matthew 6:28-34 says, And why take ye thought for raiment? Consider the lilies of the field, how they grow; they toil not, neither do they spin:

And yet I say unto you, That even Solomon in all his glory was not arrayed like one of these.

Wherefore, if God so clothe the grass of the field, which to day is,

and to morrow is cast into the oven, shall he not much more clothe you, O ye of little faith?

Therefore take no thought, saying, What shall we eat? or, What shall we drink? or, Wherewithal shall we be clothed

(For after all these things do the Gentiles seek:) for your heavenly Father knoweth that ye have need of all these things.

But seek ye first the kingdom of God, and his righteousness; and all these things shall be added unto you.

Take therefore no thought for the morrow: for the morrow shall take thought for the things of itself. Sufficient unto the day is the evil thereof.

Multiple times in these scriptures we see the words, "Take no thought." How do you take a fear or worry thought? The answer is by NOT resisting the thought. We don't have to take every thought that we think. If we do take a thought, it will ultimately get into your heart, and what gets into your heart will start coming out of your mouth as well. You will start talking your fear and worry because out of the abundance of the heart the mouth speaks! Jesus said, "Take no thought saying..." We have to be reminded that the Lord already knows our needs, so we don't have to fear and take any worry or fear-based thoughts. I like how the Living Bible translates this passage.

And why worry about your clothes? Look at the field lilies! They don't worry about theirs.

Yet King Solomon in all his glory was not clothed as beautifully as they.

And if God cares so wonderfully for flowers that are here today and gone tomorrow, won't he more surely care for you, O men of little faith?

So don't worry at all about having enough food and clothing. Why be like the heathen? For they take pride in all these things and are deeply concerned about them. But your heavenly Father already knows perfectly well that you need them,

and he will give them to you if you give him first place in your life and live as he wants you to.

So don't be anxious about tomorrow. God will take care of your tomorrow too. Live one day at a time.

We are to be seeking God first and focused on Him at all times. This means every morning and evening being focused and in faith, resisting the enemy and all his fears, worries, and all of his fearful thoughts! The enemy is all about us taking and receiving his thoughts of fear and worry so he can steal the peace of God in our lives until we become depressed and discouraged. I'll end with these two scriptures.

"But seek ye first the kingdom of God, and his righteousness; and all these things shall be added unto you" (Matthew 6:33).

It's obvious Jesus wants us to seek Him first in everything we do. A Bible story that paints this picture of seeking God first is when Mary chose to sit and hear the Word at Jesus' feet instead of anything else.

As Jesus and the disciples continued on their way to Jerusalem they came to a village where a woman named Martha welcomed them into her home.

Her sister Mary sat on the floor, listening to Jesus as he talked.

But Martha was the jittery type and was worrying over the big dinner she was preparing. She came to Jesus and said, "Sir, doesn't it seem unfair to you that my sister just sits here while I do all the work? Tell her to come and help me."

But the Lord said to her, "Martha, dear friend, you are so upset over all these details!

There is really only one thing worth being concerned about. Mary has discovered it—and I won't take it away from her!" **(Luke 10:38-42 TLB).**

I think what sticks out most to me in this story is NOT that Martha was busy preparing a meal. What's wrong with making sure everything was ready and prepared for company, and not just any company, but Jesus? Martha missed the most important thing. When Jesus started talking, she was busy and worried instead of doing what Mary did. When Jesus was talking, she stopped and sat on the floor to receive the Word. Wow! How often do we need to just stop and listen to God's Word instead of doing this and doing that!

This is how we seek the Kingdom first! We are not to seek things and be worried about things. We seek God, and all the things will be added to us. In other words, if we put God first and His Word, everything else we need will come our way. This is what peace looks like. It looks like a person that is seeking Jesus first and believing everything else will fall into place. We just need to keep our mind stayed on the Lord, and we will live in peace.

"You will keep *him* in perfect peace, *Whose* mind *is* stayed *on You,* Because he trusts in You" (Isaiah 26:3 NKJV).

CHAPTER 3

THE WAR IN THE MIND

The battle in our thought life is a battle for our mind. It's the battle between our ears that makes all the difference in the world. Satan knows to attack our thought life because the thoughts we choose will determine defeat or victory in our lives. The thoughts we embrace or reject make all the difference to our lives. We never really think of the war between our ears and the intense grappling match that is occurring at all times of the day and night. Thoughts coming from out of nowhere! The good news is, no matter the thoughts, you can control your thought life. In this chapter, I'm going to teach you how to control your thought life. One of the first scriptures I learned when I got born again was **2 Corinthians 10:4-5**. Let's take a look at this scripture as God shows us how to control our thought life.

The Warfare Is a Fight for the Mind

"(For the weapons of our warfare are not carnal, but mighty through God to the pulling down of strong

holds;) Casting down imaginations, and every high thing that exalteth itself against the knowledge of God, and bringing into captivity every thought to the obedience of Christ" (2 Corinthians 10:4-5 KJV).

God knew the war was going to be in our minds so He equipped us to be able to win in our thought life. We have mighty weapons that are able to defeat every thought from the evil one that enters our thought life. Just think, God called us to fight. Not a carnal fight, but a spiritual fight. It's obvious there is a spiritual warfare going on. God wants us to take fearful thoughts captive or prisoner, or they will take us captive or prisoner. Thoughts not cast down ultimately produce strongholds in our lives.

We have weapons for warfare. The Greek definition of the word *warfare* is taken from the word *stratos*. The word *stratos* we get from the English word *strategy*. This tells me that spiritual warfare is not on accident but is something that is strategically planned. The enemy has a strategy to fight us and attack us. Satan is after our minds and he's very strategic in how he does that. Just think, before the battle even begins, Satan is strategizing how he's going to try to trip you up and create a stronghold in your mind. He's well-planned and has been watching us for a long time remembering our failures. He will come back with the same temptations just packaged in different ways. He's going to do this through thoughts. His attacks will be in your mind and your thought life.

The good news about this mental warfare is that Jesus equipped His church to win the battle of the mind. We also have a strategy in warfare. Our weapons are not carnal but strong and powerful to be able to defeat any attack of our enemy. We have mighty weapons! Our weapons are full of God's power and might! We can demolish any thought that comes against the knowledge of God.

Paul is clear in the writing of **2 Corinthians 10:4-5**, that we have a part to play in the fight. We are to cast down the wrong thoughts. God is not going to cast the thoughts down for us. What does it mean to cast down thoughts? Let's look at the J. B. Phillips translation of this verse.

Demolishing Thoughts Against the Word

> "The very weapons we use are not those of human warfare but powerful in God's warfare for the destruction of the enemy's strongholds. Our battle is to bring down every deceptive fantasy and every imposing defence that men erect against the true knowledge of God. We even fight to capture every thought until it acknowledges the authority of Christ. Once we are sure of your obedience we shall not shrink from dealing with those who refuse to obey" (2 Corinthians 10:4-5 Phillips).

We are to cast down and bring down EVERY and ALL imaginations that are not from God. *Imaginations* comes from the word *images*. How do images get into our thought life? Satan uses thoughts to create imaginations. Some people live in constant fear because they believe the enemy's thoughts about their life, and now they imagine bad things are going to happen to them. They believe the lies of the enemy. Instead of bringing those lying thoughts from Satan into captivity, the lying thoughts begin to bring them into captivity! They may have an imagination that they are not good enough to be a child of God. So, they remain on the sidelines and never do anything for the Lord out of condemnation and guilt. That thought of not being good enough is a spirit of fear now! They didn't resist that thought so now it's a stronghold that keeps them down! Some people have a fear of crossing high bridges because they have an imagination of the bridge collapsing. This is proof that thoughts of the enemy that are not cast down turn into strongholds and fear.

Taking Authority Over Your Thoughts Requires Us Speaking to Our Thoughts

I have to be honest with you. I don't win every battle in my thought life the first time. Sometimes I lose, but I stay in the fight until I win. Casting down thoughts is giving no place to the devil in your mind. So, when a thought of evil comes across my mind, I say this out loud, "That's not my thought! I cast that thought down, right now! I refuse to give my attention to you! Get out of my thought life right now, in the Name of Jesus." We take any thought from the enemy captive! (Captive means prisoner!) I'm going to place that bad thought under arrest! If we don't take those evil thoughts captive, they will take us captive. The reason you speak to your thoughts out loud is because you don't battle thoughts with thoughts, but you battle thoughts with words.

Lastly, we must always remember that the real battle with Satan was won at the cross and the resurrection by Jesus Christ. We must approach spiritual warfare from a place of already obtained victory by Jesus Christ instead of us trying to get the victory. This is key. We are not fighting *for* victory in our thought life. We are fighting *from* victory. The blood of Jesus has already got us seated in heavenly places far above principalities!

"And hath raised us up together, and made us sit together in heavenly places in Christ Jesus" (Ephesians 2:6 KJV).

CHAPTER 4

THROW YOUR CARES ON THE LORD

In this chapter, you are going to really learn how to give God everything that has been worrying you. You will learn how to keep those thoughts of worry and fear from taking root in your life. Let's look at this life changing scripture.

"Casting all your cares [all your anxieties, all your worries, and all your concerns, once and for all] on Him, for He cares about you [with deepest affection, and watches over you very carefully]" (1 Peter 5:7 AMP).

Again, when I read this scripture, it sounds more like a command. I could see Jesus saying to me, "Kevin, I want you to cast all of your cares, anxieties and all of your worries and concerns on Me once and for all, because I care about you!" Many nights, while I laid in bed, I would have so many thoughts running through my mind about certain issues I was dealing with. I would toss and turn and struggle and let the worry choke the Word until I was in a full-blown spirit of fear. I believe the Holy Spirit led me to this verse to get me out of fear.

Once this scripture got into my heart, after I read it a thousand times it seems, I began to learn to give my worries to God. I learned to give all my fears and worries to the Father. All the things I was grappling with in my thoughts was way too much for me and was actually hurting me physically. I was experiencing burn out and maybe a chemical imbalance due to fear and worry. Just think, the whole time God was waiting to take care of it all. I've learned this about God. If you don't give Him what you're worrying about, then God's hands are tied, so to speak. The moment we cast our care onto the Lord, then God can work! God can do what He does!

As long as you keep your worry and fear in your hands, God can't work. I learned this the hard way, and I should have listened and trusted so much sooner than I did. It took me suffering and struggling with worry long enough until I came to the place I could not take it anymore. Something had to give! I gave it to Jesus! I got set free, praise God. All of those demanding thoughts were no longer grabbing my attention. I gave my care to Jesus and left it in His hands.

You and I are not that big that we can handle every life issue without the help of the Lord. I don't know about you, but I don't want to face any issue or problem without the Lord. God tells us to cast our care on Him. Cast our worries and anxieties on Him. So how do we cast our care on Him? There are many ways I do it that allows me to keep my peace in the middle of the storm.

Definition of Casting

The Greek definition of the word *cast* in this verse means, "to throw upon." This is not a casual action. It is a deliberate, forceful throwing like throwing an enemy down to the ground. This scripture paints a picture that as soon as worry comes, we are to give it to God with forceful, rapid movement. We are to be fast about it. Why? Because worry is a form of fear and fear is a form of anxiety. Many times, we end up fighting anxiety because we are not casting our care but carrying our care. The Lord wants us to be in the habit of giving every situation to Him every day of our life, until we leave this earth and go to heaven. Our Heavenly Father wants us to give Him every worry! Worry is anything we haven't given to God. If you are worried about it, then you have not cast your care on the Lord.

When my daughter turned eighteen years old, she decided to move out in the middle of the night to chase after a boy. The Holy Spirit woke me up to find her packed and ready to leave. I didn't even know she had a boyfriend. My heart was shattered, and there was nothing I could do to stop her from walking out the door. Three dudes pulled up down the street from my house, and I watched my daughter walk down the sidewalk to get in the car with three strange guys I had never met. They were very, very smart by not pulling up in my driveway because I had taken my pastor's hat off and put on my warrior hat.

I was devastated and full of fear of what would happen to my only child. I allowed the enemy to beat me up for months. It was very traumatizing as a parent to walk through this. I imagined so many different things that could be happening to my daughter. I allowed this situation to really depress me, and I allowed the spirit of fear to enter into my heart! My life would not change until I learned to cast my care once and for all onto the Lord and practice what I preached. When I would go to bed at night, I would say, "Lord, You're up all night. I'm going to sleep and let You work all of this out." I truly believed that God was working it out for good as I prayed and believed and rested in Him. It took me some time, but I finally got to the place of resting in faith.

Casting Your Cares by Confessing What You Believe

I cast my care in many ways during that time. I cast my care by opening my mouth and saying, "Father, I give You this situation. I refuse to worry about it! I cast my care onto You. I give You my daughter right now in the mighty Name of Jesus."

Then, in the process of me saying that, I would find a promise of God to say in that same sentence, and I would add on to that confession. "God, according to Your Word, You said, "And all thy children shall be taught of the Lord; and great shall be the peace of thy children" **(Isaiah 54:13 KJV**). My daughter will be taught of the Lord and will hear God and she will know the peace of God. I said this in the face of her living out of town with this dude I had never met. This is what faith does in the middle of the storm. Faith speaks!

Refuse to Take Back the Worry

Once I cast the care on the Lord, I refused to worry about it. My dad, Curtis, taught me this when I was about nineteen years old. He would say, "Son, cast your care on the Lord, but don't take it out of His hands by worrying about it." When you and I are worried about anything in life, then it's in our hands. So, my big lesson in this was to keep the problems out of my hands and in the Lord's hands. Think about it like this. When we don't cast our cares, we in essence are saying to God, "I can do better with this situation than You can, God." I believe as long as you are concerned, worried and in fear, you are in God's way of working things out! It's not until we give it to the Lord that God can get involved in the problem.

My daughter came home one year later after I learned to cast my care on the Lord. I allowed the enemy to torment me, when in the Name of Jesus, I had power and authority over every thought of the enemy. We allow the enemy to bully us all the time when we have the ability to put a stop to the enemy and his attacks. This is why I'm writing this book. I don't want the enemy to bully you! We are NOT to be bullied by a defeated foe!

God never intended on us living our life full of burdens and carrying the heavy load. In this scripture Jesus gives us a picture of living life free of worry and burdens that would weigh us down. We are commanded to rest in Jesus. How do we do that? We stop worry in its tracks by immediately casting our cares upon Jesus. Jesus says:

"Come to Me, all who are weary and heavily burdened [by religious rituals that provide no peace], and I will give you rest [refreshing your souls with salvation]. Take My yoke upon you and learn from Me [following Me as My disciple], for I am gentle and humble in heart, and YOU WILL FIND REST [renewal, blessed quiet] FOR YOUR SOULS. For My yoke is easy [to bear] and My burden is light" (Mathew 11:28-30 AMP).

Wow! If we come to the Lord when we are burdened, He promises us that we will find rest in Him. Resting in the Lord is when we know we are in faith. All hell can be breaking loose all around us, but we can still be resting, casting our cares, having no worries, and not yielding to fear. I want to end this chapter with a confession of what we believe. Remember, we can't fight thoughts with thoughts. We fight thoughts with words. Say this confession out loud:

Father, I cast the whole care of this situation (name the issue here) and any other issues that might arise in my life this day onto You, Lord. I refuse to take it back out of Your hands. I put all of my trust in You, Lord, and I believe that You will turn this situation around for my good, in Jesus' mighty Name. I declare that my days of worry are over! I stop worry in its tracks in the powerful Name of Jesus! I refuse to allow the enemy to get me in fear in Jesus' Name!

CHAPTER 5

DON'T LET YOUR HEART BE TROUBLED

I don't think there is anything more difficult than a troubled heart. A troubled heart is a worried and anxious heart! Jesus knew He would be going to the cross to be crucified and punished for our sins. Jesus began to prepare His disciples' hearts by telling them that there were going to be some difficult times ahead, and that He must go to the Father. I'm sure His disciples were confused and really hurt by this announcement. Pain must have gripped their hearts, but Jesus made sure that they were comforted with these words:

> **"Let not your heart be troubled: ye believe in God, believe also in me" (John 14:1 KJV).**

> **"Do not let your heart be troubled (afraid, cowardly). Believe [confidently] in God *and* trust in Him, [have faith, hold on to it, rely on it, keep going and] believe also in Me" (John 14:1 AMP).**

Jesus knew there was trouble ahead, and He knew that His disciples' hearts would be assaulted by the enemy and gripped with fear and worry. Jesus spoke encouragement to them to prepare them for the future! Jesus told them, "Don't let your heart be troubled." The word *troubled* is the Greek word *taresso*, which means "to shake, to trouble, to disquiet, to unsettle, to perplex, to cause anxiety, or even to cause feelings of grief." It is the picture of somebody feeling inwardly shaken, unsettled, confused, and upset. Have you ever felt this way before?

"Let not your heart be troubled." Those words helped me many nights lying in bed with so much going on in my life. I would say over and over out loud, "My heart is not troubled." Jesus told me that my heart should NOT be troubled. I'm sticking with what Jesus said. I am not troubled, anxious or grieved. I will not let what's happening in my life trouble me. I am NOT a troubled man, nor will I allow Satan to trouble me.

Now, the psalmist David said, "What time I am afraid, I will trust in thee. In God I will praise his word, in God I have put my trust; I will not fear what flesh can do unto me" (Psalm 56:3-4).

Let me tell you there are going to be difficult times where you are just going to have to say, "Well God, this is how I feel, but I'm not moved by my feelings. I trust in You!" Trusting God is a decision, not a feeling. So many bad decisions have been made in the middle of a troubled situation when people's feelings got in the way. We were never meant to be led by our feelings but by the Spirit of God.

What has been troubling you lately? Is it your children? Is it your future? finances? social issues? physical problems? or mental issues? What has stolen the peace from your heart and left you with worry and fear and confusion? You have authority over your own heart and whether you allow fear to enter it or not. It's your call not God's. In John chapter 14 Jesus said again, "Don't let your heart be troubled."

"Peace I leave with you, my peace I give unto you: not as the world giveth, give I unto you. Let not your heart be troubled, neither let it be afraid" (John 14:27).

A Troubled Heart Is a Fearful Heart

"Let not your heart be troubled, neither let it be afraid." This time Jesus said, "Don't let your heart be troubled and don't let it be afraid." He is saying, "Don't do it. Don't be troubled and don't allow fear into your heart." You and I have an invitation to enter into His rest and receive His peace. Don't base it on feelings. Receive it by faith. I have walked through some of the most difficult times in my life with chaos around me but peace in my heart. Then there have been times I allowed my peace to go right out that door and allowed fear and anxiety right back in.

Thank God, He's given me His peace. Jesus is my peace-giver. I receive His peace by faith. I receive His rest, and I trust Him.

I'm fixing my thoughts and my mind around the Word of God. Then I keep my mind on Him and what He says — not on the problem. We need to make sure we slow down the pace to receive that peace. Slow down and get into the Word and prayer and watch what God will do for you. You will enter a place of rest and you will walk in His peace.

I'll end with this verse for you and me. "And the peace of God, which surpasses all understanding, will guard your hearts and minds through Christ Jesus" (Philippians 4:7 NKJV).

I have the peace of God, and it doesn't matter if I don't understand how God is going to get me through what I'm going through. I trust Him. If it's not God who you're trusting, then it's going to be yourself, it's going to be your friends, the government, the world, your bank account, your employer. All of those things are shaky and very unstable, but God is not. He is the one thing that is never shaken. That's why the Bible refers to Him as the Rock. He's a rock that cannot be moved.

CHAPTER 6

FAITH VS. FEAR

We really only have these two options in life. We are going to choose to live by faith or live by our fears. The choice is ours! I will describe what fear and faith are in this chapter so you and I can better understand the meaning of faith and fear.

The Forbidden Fears

Let's talk about fear. I found out that the worst liars in the world are your own fears. I promise you this: if I had listened to my fears, I would not be in the ministry. I would not have started a church. I would not be writing this book. I would not be preaching. In everything God has called me to do in my life, there has always been a presence of fear. The first time I ever shared my testimony on the radio I had so much fear. When they put the microphone in front of me, I ran out of the radio station in fear. The woman that was interviewing me came outside to find me and said, "Kevin, if you don't do this, you may never do this. You must overcome your fear!" I went back in there and shared my testimony, and now I have been on the radio more times than I can count.

Two Kinds of Fears

There are two kinds of fear. The first fear is a healthy fear of the Lord that causes us to respect and honor God. The second fear is the forbidden fear, simply defined as, "a dread, uneasiness, or anxiousness." This fear is an evil fear that comes to rob us of God's peace and rest in our lives. This forbidden fear is the "fear nots" in the Bible. "Fear not" and "be not afraid" appears in the Bible well over 180 times. I think God is telling us to FEAR NOT!

There are so many fears and phobias on planet Earth today. These fears paralyze you and cause anxiety and panic. The Word of God teaches us that fear is more than a feeling, it is a spirit.

2 Timothy 1:7 says, "God hath not given us the spirit of fear; but of power, and of love, and of a sound mind."

Fear is fed through your intellect, and then goes down into your spirit. This is how people are ruled by the spirit of fear.

Remember, fear is not natural to the believer. It comes from the outside in. God is not the author of fear! Satan is the author of fear! He's the one behind every fear, and we need to remember that God didn't give us a spirit of fear. Fear is a wide-open door for Satan to come and wreak havoc on our minds.

When I was in my twenties, I was surfing Playalinda Beach in Titusville, Florida. I was waiting for the next set of waves to come through. As I was sitting on my surfboard, I could hear one of my friend's voices in the background yelling, "Kevin! Kevin! Shark!" I looked to my right and there was a six foot shark already beside me. The shark hit my leg, turned me and my surfboard a whole 180 degrees, and then took his tail and splashed me in the face. I immediately laid flat on my surfboard. I was paralyzed with fear, and I did not even have time to get my scream out. I tried, but I could not even scream. I began to paddle to the beach with my fingertips until a wave came through. I caught that wave and made it to the beach where I cried and thanked God for His protection. That experience could have left me scarred and scared for life. I remember the next time I went surfing the fear was there, but I had a scripture ready to confess over my life. Now don't get me wrong. If I see a shark before I paddle out, the "sound mind" in me says, "It's not a good day to surf."

Definition of Fear

Let's talk about what fear is. There are so many different definitions, but I think what describes fear best is this, "Fear is faith in reverse or perverted faith." We know faith means to believe, but fear is believing as well. What is faith? Faith is taking God at His Word and believing you receive what He says in His word. Fear is taking the devil at his word and what he says. If you are afraid of frogs and actually believe that those frogs could harm you, then you are still believing! It's faith in reverse. We have no time doing life in reverse and living in fear. Let's get our faith in God's Word and move forward. A good story of faith versus fear is found in **Mark chapter 5:21-24.**

And when Jesus was passed over again by ship unto the other side, much people gathered unto him: and he was nigh unto the sea.

And, behold, there cometh one of the rulers of the synagogue, Jairus by name; and when he saw him, he fell at his feet,

And besought him greatly, saying, My little daughter lieth at the point of death: I pray thee, come and lay thy hands on her, that she may be healed; and she shall live.

And Jesus went with him; and much people followed him, and thronged him.

I want to point out in this scripture that this man's daughter is on her death bed, but Jairus speaks his faith. He says, "If You lay hands on her, she will be healed." That's how faith talks! When Jesus heard him speak those words, Jesus went with him. I love that! Faith brings Jesus on your journey no matter what you're going through! Let's continue reading the story in **Mark 5:25-34:**

> **And a certain woman, which had an issue of blood twelve years,**
>
> **And had suffered many things of many physicians, and had spent all that she had, and was nothing bettered, but rather grew worse,**
>
> **When she had heard of Jesus, came in the press behind, and touched his garment.**
>
> **For she said, If I may touch but his clothes, I shall be whole.**
>
> **And straightway the fountain of her blood was dried up; and she felt in her body that she was healed of that plague.**
>
> **And Jesus, immediately knowing in himself that virtue had gone out of him, turned him about in the press, and said, Who touched my clothes?**

And his disciples said unto him, Thou seest the multitude thronging thee, and sayest thou, Who touched me?

And he looked round about to see her that had done this thing.

But the woman fearing and trembling, knowing what was done in her, came and fell down before him, and told him all the truth.

And he said unto her, Daughter, thy faith hath made thee whole; go in peace, and be whole of thy plague.

This must have been very hard for Jairus knowing his daughter is at the point of death, and here comes this woman with an issue of blood that's not even supposed to be in the synagogue touching Jesus. Jesus stopped in His tracks because someone touched Him with their faith! This woman confessed it was her, and she also confessed what she believed! She believed that if she touched Jesus' garment, she would be healed! I want to point out Jesus' response to faith. Jairus' faith caused Jesus to come with him to his daughter, and this woman's faith stopped Jesus in His tracks. So many people were touching Jesus, but He only felt one touch and that was the woman who had faith. Let's continue reading in **verse 35:**

> **While he yet spake, there came from the ruler of the synagogue's house certain which said, Thy daughter is dead: why troublest thou the Master any further?**

Here comes fear! Fear always says, "It's over! Stop believing in healing! Stop believing that Jesus can do miracles." Fear will always attack your faith in action! It will be in the middle of trusting God. It will be in the middle of you walking on water! The waves will demand your attention! Fear shows up with all its lies and tries to get your faith to go in reverse. **Verse 36 says:**

> **As soon as Jesus heard the word that was spoken, he saith unto the**

ruler of the synagogue, Be not afraid, only believe.

Jesus shows us how we are to deal with fear in this verse. Jesus, in essence, was saying, "Don't turn your faith off! Just believe!" The only responsibility we have is to believe! Now this could have been a different story! Jairus could have been offended at this woman for stopping Jesus and could have believed the lie that his daughter was dead! Jesus stopped fear in its tracks! **Mark 5:37-40 says:**

And he suffered no man to follow him, save Peter, and James, and John the brother of James.

And he cometh to the house of the ruler of the synagogue, and seeth the tumult, and them that wept and wailed greatly.

And when he was come in, he saith unto them, Why make ye this ado, and weep? the damsel is not dead, but sleepeth.

And they laughed him to scorn. But when he had put them all out, he taketh the father and the mother of the damsel, and them that were with him, and entereth in where the damsel was lying.

These people laughed at Jesus! They laughed because he believed she was not dead! They laughed at Jesus' faith! People always laugh at faith people. I love how Jesus kicked all the doubt and fear out of the house! Maybe it's time we kick fear out of our house! Maybe it's time we just tell the enemy, "My house is not your playground anymore!"

Mark 5:41-43 says, And he took the damsel by the hand, and said unto her, Talitha cumi; which is, being interpreted, Damsel, I say unto thee, arise.

And straightway the damsel arose, and walked; for she was of the age of twelve years. And they were astonished with a great astonishment.

And he charged them straitly that no man should know it; and commanded that something should be given her to eat.

This was a great illustration of faith vs fear. Fear didn't win in these people's lives! They had faith! They had confidence in Jesus to get it done and so do we! We know Jesus is still healing, still delivering, still doing miracles! Whatever you are facing, "Be not afraid, only believe!"

CHAPTER 7

DON'T YOU CARE?

This chapter is dedicated to those who feel that God doesn't care for them. I'm talking about believers. This is one of the number one weapons the enemy uses to get us into fear and dread. He convinces us that God doesn't care! You're not the only one who has ever felt that way. Even Jesus' disciples felt that way in **Mark 4:35-38.**

> **And the same day, when the even was come, he saith unto them, Let us pass over unto the other side.**
>
> **And when they had sent away the multitude, they took him even as he was in the ship. And there were also with him other little ships.**
>
> **And there arose a great storm of wind, and the waves beat into the ship, so that it was now full.**
>
> **And he was in the hinder part of the ship, asleep on a pillow.**

I'm in awe how Jesus was sleeping in the storm with a boat full of water. Going to sleep in a storm could be a difficult task, but not for a faith person! Going to sleep can be one of the most spiritual things a person does. Worried and fearful people stay up all night focusing on the problem. How could Jesus sleep in the middle of a storm and a boat full of water? The answer is, Jesus believed in what He said. **"Let us pass over unto the other side."** The disciples could have believed that as well.

Mark 4:38 says, "and they awake him, and say unto him, Master, carest thou not that we perish?" In the Living Bible it says, **"Jesus was asleep at the back of the boat with his head on a cushion. Frantically they wakened him, shouting, 'Teacher, don't you even care that we are all about to drown?'"**

Here it is! The disciples were surely showing their lack of faith to make it to the other side. They had a chance to say, "Jesus, You said we are going to the other side and this storm is not going to stop us!" They had a chance to go over there where Jesus was sleeping and lay down next Him! They could have said, "Jesus walks on water. He doesn't sink, and if He doesn't sink, then we won't sink." That's not what they did! They questioned if Jesus really cared if they perished, drowned or died. That boat was not only full of water, but it was also full of worry, fear and anxiety.

So many times in life we do what the disciples did. We get concerned and question if Jesus is up in heaven sleeping on a pillow and wonder why God hasn't intervened in our situation. When the whole time God has given us the authority over every storm. We have the ability to fall asleep with no fear or worry in our hearts. In the midst of a bad report, we can rest and have no fear. In the middle of the storm, we can still know Jesus is in our boat and that's all that matters.

Mark 4:39-41 says, "And he arose, and rebuked the wind, and said unto the sea, Peace, be still. And the wind ceased, and there was a great calm. And he said unto them, Why are ye so fearful? how is it that ye have no faith? And they feared exceedingly, and said one to another,

What manner of man is this, that even the wind and the sea obey him?"

Speak to Your Storm

Finally, Jesus shows us how to deal with the storm. He spoke to the storm! He questioned why they were so fearful! The disciples had their eyes on the water filling the boat, the winds, and the waves while they could have acted just like Jesus and spoken to the storm! I challenge all of us to go to sleep in faith! Speak to the storms you're facing and declare peace over that storm. Jesus is a master of taking us from a great storm to a great calm, but that only happens when we get out of fear and into faith.

When the disciples feared and questioned if God cared for them, they were really questioning the love of God. Fear is really a fear that God doesn't love you enough to protect you or provide for you. The Word of God says there is no fear in love.

1 John 4:18 says, "There is no fear in love; but perfect love casteth out fear: because fear hath torment. He that feareth is not made perfect in love."

Believe in the Love of God

Fear is a tormentor, and the way we overcome fear is by God's love. We must believe and receive the love of God, and we must give God's love to others. Fear can't torment me if I know God cares for me, loves me, and I give that care and love to others. This is literally how fear is cast out and flushed out of our lives. We should say throughout each day, "My God loves me, I love Him, and I will love others." This is another weapon in the war on fear! We should be conscious of God's love daily in our lives. When we get this revelation of God's love, it will chase fear and insecurity right out of our lives.

What is stopping you from believing and receiving the love of God? Is it the hurts and wounds of the past? Is it guilt and shame that you grapple with? Is it your insecurities or low self-esteem? When you have a lack of knowledge of the love of God, fear will keep you bound in guilt and shame. It will keep you bound by insecurity. When the love of God shows up in your life, it will flush out all fear and you will experience freedom for the first time in a long time. That freedom can and will last forever.

CHAPTER 8

TEACH ME HOW TO FIGHT

One of the first things I learned as a kid growing up in Pulaski, Tennessee, is how to fight. Fighting is what we did as kids. My brother and I were known for fighting. My brother would even set up fights with other neighborhood kids, and we would meet up and scrap it out. I won most of my fights and would say I was pretty good at it. Even now I train Brazilian jiu jitsu and am still learning how to fight. Why am I sharing this with you? Well, if you didn't know this already, in life we are going to have to learn how to fight. Every aspect of God's plan for our lives requires faith. However, wherever faith is required, a fight will be involved. This fight I'm talking about is not a physical fight like when I was growing up. It's a different kind of war! I want to teach you how I fight now and how you can fight as well. The Word talks about who we are fighting and who we are not fighting.

"For we wrestle not against flesh and blood, but against principalities, against powers, against the rulers of the darkness of this world, against spiritual

**wickedness in high places"
(Ephesians 6:12).**

Our battle is not with each other but with principalities and rulers of darkness and wickedness in high places. Fear is not a physical fight but a spiritual fight. I'm going to teach you how God showed me how to fight and win those spiritual battles. The first thing I learned in my walk with God was to fight every battle with my faith. You and I have to become faith fighters and fight against fear.

Fight with Your Faith

If you have lived any length of time, you know that it takes faith to make it in the world we live in. So many things are thrown at us each day that we will either fight with our faith or live in our fears. The Bible tells us to fight the good fight of faith! It's good that you're fighting! We ought to be fighting off fear and worry and anxiety. We ought to be in the fight of faith resisting all forms of fear that the enemy brings against us. Let's look at these scriptures about the fight of faith.

"Fight the good fight of faith, lay hold on eternal life, to which you were also called and have confessed the good confession in the presence of many witnesses. I urge you in the sight of God who gives life to all things, and before Christ Jesus who witnessed the good confession before Pontius Pilate" (1 Timothy 6:12-13 NKJV).

How Do We Fight with Our Faith

We are told to fight the good fight of faith. How do we fight with our faith? How did Jesus fight with His faith? Verse 13 tells us Jesus stood before Pontius Pilate and confessed His faith! Can you imagine the crowd wanting Jesus to be crucified and demanding Pontius Pilate to do it? All because Jesus didn't back down with His confession! I'm sure fear was present, but Jesus did not hesitate to say who He was! This is how we fight! We don't back down, and we stand up to any situation with our confession of God's Word. We confess who we are in Christ! We confess that we believe in the death and resurrection of Jesus! We confess the promises of God in the face of fear! Jesus was truly the faith fighter's champion of all time! Now we can fight with our faith! We fight with the Word of God in our mouth. That's how we fight.

In 2 Timothy 4:7 (KJV) it says, "I have fought a good fight, I have finished my course, I have kept the faith."

Paul lived a life of faith to his final departure. He finished his course! Don't we all want to say those words, "I have finished my course"? Don't we want to say that we have lived our lives by walking by faith to our very last breath on this earth? That's my plan! I wrote this book to encourage you to never give up! I want to encourage you to fight and keep your faith and finish your course in this life kicking dirt in the devil's face.

Now we know how to fight with our faith by keeping the Word of God in our mouths. It's time we begin to know the

Word of God on a deeper level than just Sunday church. Overcoming your fears and worries and anxieties is all about replacing them with the promises of God. How can we overcome and win this war on fear if we don't have anything to replace fear with? How are we going to stop allowing the lies of the enemy to overtake our thought life if we don't know God's truth? We are going to flood our hearts with the Word of God, that's how!

We get the Word in our hearts and in our mouths so we can fight off anything that comes our way in this life. How do you get the Word in your heart? You meditate on the scriptures and read them aloud daily over your life. When you do this, you will start to take faith over fear, healing over sickness, rest over stress, and peace over strife. Faith comes by hearing the Word of God, and fear comes by hearing the devil's lies. The more we hear God's Word, the more we build our faith. The Word of God is faith food. If you need faith, you will get faith from the Word of God.

Romans 10:17 (NKJV) says, "So then faith comes by hearing, and hearing by the word of God." Faith comes by hearing, and hearing, and hearing God's Word. This is how faith comes into your heart.

Fear, on the other hand, comes by hearing and hearing the devil's lies. When it comes to fear and worry, there are hundreds of scriptures in the Bible that can build your faith. I'm going to repeat the scriptures I shared with you in the book in chapter ten because those are the scriptures I meditated on daily until I could drive my fears away! So now you can be fully equipped to face any fear or worry. I'm going to list some categories where I used my faith in God's Word to overcome my fears. Once you have a promise, then you can begin to replace your fears with faith in the Word instead of perverted faith in Satan's lies. I have decided to give you some of my go-to scriptures on some areas I struggled in and how I overcame them.

CHAPTER 9

GET OUT OF THE BOAT

This chapter is all about taking the steps of faith and overcoming your fears. By now it is my hope that you are refusing to fear and recognizing fear as your strongest enemy! Now you're ready to step out in faith and overcome every fear in your life. Just know I have grappled with so many fears over the years, and there will be a moment you will have to step out in faith!

I remember, when I first started attending church, they taught about tithing. I was very confused about what the tithe meant and why we did it. I was only nineteen years old, and giving a tenth of all my income was very scary especially since I didn't have a lot of money. I had to step out of the boat and trust God with money. I found out years later, if God could trust me with money, He would keep putting money in my hands. Now I'm in my fifties and I'm still tithing and giving whatever the Holy Spirit tells me to above the tithe. There is nothing more fun than stepping out and living the life of faith. Let's look at Peter, one of Jesus' disciples, and how he stepped out of the boat in faith in **Matthew 14:22-33.**

> **And straightway Jesus constrained his disciples to get into a ship, and to go before him unto the other side, while he sent the multitudes away.**
>
> **And when he had sent the multitudes away, he went up into a mountain apart to pray: and when the evening was come, he was there alone.**
>
> **But the ship was now in the midst of the sea, tossed with waves: for the wind was contrary.**
>
> **And in the fourth watch of the night Jesus went unto them, walking on the sea.**
>
> **And when the disciples saw him walking on the sea, they were troubled, saying, It is a spirit; and they cried out for fear.**

But straightway Jesus spake unto them, saying, Be of good cheer; it is I; be not afraid.

And Peter answered him and said, Lord, if it be thou, bid me come unto thee on the water.

And he said, Come. And when Peter was come down out of the ship, he walked on the water, to go to Jesus.

But when he saw the wind boisterous, he was afraid; and beginning to sink, he cried, saying, Lord, save me.

And immediately Jesus stretched forth his hand, and caught him, and said unto him, O thou of little faith, wherefore didst thou doubt?

And when they were come into the ship, the wind ceased.

Then they that were in the ship came and worshipped him, saying, Of a truth thou art the Son of God.

I believe Jesus is calling all of us to get out of the boat. I have made some game-changing moves over the years where we had to be like Peter and get out of the boat. One thing I learned: as long as I had a Word from God to step out, then regardless of the fears, I could do anything my Father told me to. I just refused to give into the fear and allow fear to keep me in the boat. I knew there were waves, so to speak, but I got faith in the Word of God.

When Terri and I started Faith City Church many years ago, I can remember the fear like yesterday! I was lying in bed one morning when we were gearing up for our first service. I opened my eyes and I felt Satan in my room. If I could describe what Satan feels like, I would say the spirit of fear. Then I heard these lies in my head. "You are a loser, and this is all going to fail. You're going nowhere. No one is going to go to your church. You're not smart enough. You don't have enough money. You don't have enough team members." Lie after lie!

I remember telling Satan to get out of my room. I had a Word from God, and I was getting out of the boat! If you don't get out of the boat, you can't walk on water. I can honestly say we have ministered to thousands of people over the years. I can tell you there have been so many people born again in that church, and every time it happened to somebody, I would just thank the Lord that He called me out of the boat.

Speak to the Fear

How do you get out of the boat? You have to first do what Jesus did. Jesus spoke to fear! Jesus said, "Be not afraid!" You might want to say that right now, "Be NOT afraid!" When the disciples heard Jesus' voice, it silenced their fears. Fear needs to hear Jesus' voice in your mouth.

And he said, Come. And when Peter was come down out of the ship, he walked on the water, to go to Jesus.

But when he saw the wind boisterous, he was afraid; and beginning to sink, he cried, saying, Lord, save me.

And immediately Jesus stretched forth his hand, and caught him, and said unto him, O thou of little faith, wherefore didst thou doubt?

And when they were come into the ship, the wind ceased.

Then they that were in the ship came and worshipped him, saying, Of a truth thou art the Son of God. (Matthew 14:29-33).

Refuse to Focus on the Circumstances

The next thing we do when we get out of the boat is refuse to get our eyes on the circumstances. They will demand your attention! The winds and waves will always be there when you step out and obey God on anything. We see what happens when we get into fear! We will always sink when we get our eyes off of the Word of God. I know this about Jesus. He doesn't sink, and if He doesn't sink, then I don't sink if I have my eyes on Him. The only time we sink in fear is when we believe the winds and waves over Jesus' voice.

CHAPTER 10

GIVE FAITH A VOICE

I wanted this chapter to go last because I'm going to be giving you some scriptures to read and speak over your life and the situations you may be facing. Now we know how to fight with our faith and how to release our faith. We are going to talk about the power of words.

I learned many years ago that faith is voice activated. Since the COVID-19 years, we rarely see water faucets in public restrooms that have on and off knobs. They are motion activated! If you don't put your hand under the faucet and create motion, nothing happens, and no water will come out. Our faith is voice activated! If you don't speak to the mountain, the mountain won't move! We can have faith, but we must learn to release our faith with our words. The first scripture I ever memorized in the Bible was found in **Mark 11:23.**

> **"For verily I say unto you, That whosoever shall say unto this mountain, Be thou removed, and be thou cast into the sea; and shall not doubt in his heart, but shall**

believe that those things which he saith shall come to pass; he shall have whatsoever he saith."

Jesus cursed a fig tree that bore no fruit, and the following day His disciples noticed that the fig tree had withered away. In response to their surprise, Jesus taught them about faith. Jesus responded with whoever speaks to a mountain and shall not doubt in his heart, shall have what he says. This is a spiritual principle that changed my life forever. I learned from Jesus that it matters what I speak out of my mouth. Jesus encourages us to speak to things! Speak to problems and speak to your worries and fears! Speak to your body and even the organs inside of your body.

When I was nineteen, I began to confess the Word of God out of my mouth and started speaking to the mountains in my life. Jesus gave His faith a voice by speaking to the fig tree which withered from its roots. He taught that our faith has the potential to do the same, not just to curse a fig tree, but also to move a mountain. Faith must move our mouths to speak before it will move or impact anything else in our lives. Our faith must be voiced!

Jesus spoke to a fig tree. Jesus spoke to sick bodies and demon-possessed individuals. If Jesus used His faith and spoke, then I believe we ought to use our faith and speak! Every time I encounter something difficult in my life, I find the promises of God and load up on them. Then, I begin to speak to the problems. We can aim our mouths in the direction we want our lives to go. You can aim your mouth in the direction you want your body to go, your finances, or your future.

Jesus wants us to speak to the mountain the way He spoke to the fig tree. If we don't speak to the mountains in our lives, the mountains won't move. We can speak to our fears and our worries, and we have God-given authority to speak! That's how powerful our speech is. We can speak in faith to any situation, no matter how big or small it may appear to be. Words create; therefore, words can dismantle.

Here are some promises that I have used over the years in certain areas of my own life, and I have listed them for you! I like to start with the promise of God and then confess the promise in the area where there's a struggle. Here are some of my confessions from my own personal struggles. I'm sure most of them will be a huge blessing to your life.

SPEAKING TO YOUR MOUNTAIN

Promises for Your Children

Isaiah 54:13 (NKJV), "All your children *shall be* **taught by the LORD, And great** *shall be* **the peace of your children."**

Say this: "My child will be taught of the Lord, and he/she will have God's peace. My child will NOT be taught by the devil, he/she will be taught by the Lord. He/she will not listen to the voice of a stranger and will hear from heaven in Jesus' Name."

Isaiah 59:21 (MSG), "'As for me,' GOD says, 'this is my covenant with them: My Spirit that I've placed upon you and the words that I've given you to speak, they're not going to leave your mouths nor the mouths of your children nor the mouths of your grandchildren. You will keep repeating these words and won't ever stop.' GOD's orders."

Say this: "Satan can't steal the Word of God out of me, and He can't steal the Word of God out of my children. They shall declare God's Word and live by the

Word. Faith Wright, (put in your child's name), you are a man/woman of God, and the Word of God flows out of your mouth in Jesus' Name! The Word of God will never be stopped in my family."

Psalm 112:1-2 (AMP), "Praise the LORD! (Hallelujah!) Blessed [fortunate, prosperous, and favored by God] is the man who fears the LORD [with awe-inspired reverence and worships Him with obedience], Who delights greatly in His commandments. His descendants will be mighty on earth; The generation of the upright will be blessed."

Say this: "My child is mighty in the land and is blessed by God. (Your child's name) is blessed and highly favored by God."

Isaiah 65:23 (NKJV), "They shall not labor in vain, nor bring forth children for trouble; for they *shall be* the descendants of the blessed of the LORD, and their offspring with them."

Say this: "My child is my offspring, and my children are blessed of the Lord. I declare God's protection over (your child's name) and the blessing of Lord includes protection. My child is blessed!"

Proverbs 14:26 (TLB), "Reverence for God gives a man deep strength; his children have a place of refuge and security."

Say this: "My child finds refuge in the Lord. He/she always comes back to refuge in Jesus' Name!"

Acts 16:31-33 (KJV), "And they said, Believe on the Lord Jesus Christ, and thou shalt be saved, and thy house. And they spake unto him the word of the Lord, and to all that were in his house. And he took them the same hour of the night, and washed their stripes; and was baptized, he and all his, straightway."

Say this: "My entire house shall be saved. All my children will know Jesus and follow Jesus."

Jeremiah 29:11 (AMPC), "For I know the thoughts *and* plans I have for you, says the Lord, thoughts *and* plans for welfare *and* peace and not for evil, to give you hope in your final outcome."

Say this: "God has a plan for my child. Satan can't steal that plan. My child will live out his/her destiny. I proclaim that he/she is walking in it today. He/she is fulfilling God's plan for his/her life, and he/she has a bright future. My child will not leave the earth prematurely!"

Healing Scriptures

Psalm 103:1-5 (KJV), "Bless the LORD, O my soul: and all that is within me, bless his holy name. Bless the LORD, O my soul, and forget not all his benefits: Who forgiveth all thine iniquities; who healeth all thy diseases; Who redeemeth thy life from destruction; who crowneth thee with lovingkindness and tender mercies; Who satisfieth thy mouth with good things; so that thy youth is renewed like the eagle's."

Say this: "Jesus has healed every disease and forgives every sin! I receive healing and forgiveness today and declare that I am healed because it's part of my benefits that Jesus gave me as one of His children. His benefits are healing and forgiveness, and I receive both bought and paid for by the blood of Jesus. I am healed!"

Psalm 118:17 (KJV), "I shall not die, but live, and declare the works of the LORD."

Say this: "I will live and NOT die in the Name of Jesus! Life flows through my entire body. Life is in every organ and all of my blood in Jesus' Name! Life flows through my entire body!"

Proverbs 4:20-24 (KJV), "My son, attend to my words; incline thine ear unto my sayings. Let them not depart from thine eyes; keep them in the midst of thine heart. For they are life unto those that find them, and health to all their flesh. Keep thy heart with all diligence; for out of it are the issues of life. Put away from thee a froward mouth, and perverse lips put far from thee."

Say this: "I keep God's Word in my eyes and in my ears. God brings health to all my flesh. That includes my skin, my organs, my eyes, my ears, my legs, my back, my stomach, my heart, my knees and my mind. I speak health and healing over my entire body in Jesus' mighty Name. I command my body to be healed! I disagree with every lying symptom!"

Isaiah 53:4-5 (KJV), "Surely he hath borne our griefs, and carried our sorrows: yet we did esteem him stricken, smitten of God, and afflicted. But he was wounded for our transgressions, he was bruised for our iniquities: the chastisement of our peace was upon him; and with his stripes we are healed."

Say this: "By the stripes of Jesus, I am healed! Healed is what I am! I'm not trying to get healed; I am healed in Jesus' Name!"

Matthew 8:2-3 (KJV), "And, behold, there came a leper and worshipped him, saying, Lord, if thou wilt, thou canst make me clean. And Jesus put forth his hand, and touched him, saying, I will; be thou clean. And immediately his leprosy was cleansed."

Say this: "If Jesus had an 'I will' for this sick man, then He has an 'I will' for me. It's God's will for me to be healed, and it's God's will that I be cleansed of any disease. So, I receive and take my healing right now in Jesus' Name."

Hebrews 13:8 (KJV), "Jesus Christ the same yesterday, and to day, and for ever."

Say this: "Jesus, You healed then, and You have NOT changed. Healing belongs to me just like it did to those Jesus healed in the Gospels."

James 5:14-16 (KJV), "Is any sick among you? let him call for the elders of the church; and let them pray over him, anointing him with oil in the name of the Lord: And the prayer of faith shall save the sick, and the Lord shall raise him up; and if he have committed sins, they shall be forgiven him. Confess your faults one to another, and pray one for another, that ye may be healed. The effectual fervent prayer of a righteous man availeth much."

Say this: "I thank You, heavenly Father, for my healing and my forgiveness of sins. I pray and receive by faith my healing that was provided for me by Jesus' death and resurrection."

1 Peter 2:24 (KJV), "Who his own self bare our sins in his own body on the tree, that we, being dead to sins, should live unto righteousness: by whose stripes ye were healed."

Say this: "Jesus bore my sicknesses and diseases, and if He bore them, I don't have to bear them. By Jesus' stripes, I am healed!"

Promises for Overcoming Fear and Worry:

2 Timothy 1:7 (KJV), "For God hath not given us the spirit of fear; but of power, and of love, and of a sound mind."

Say this: "I refuse to fear in Jesus' Name! I slam the door to every fear right now that I'm facing. I will not yield to fear, and I will not receive the spirit of fear. I have a sound mind! I have the mind of Christ. Satan can't have my mind! Spirit of fear, I rebuke you, in the Name of Jesus. I cast you out of my mind and out of my life."

Hebrews 10:23 (KJV), "Let us hold fast the profession of our faith without wavering; (for he is faithful that promised.)"
Say this: "If I worry, then I waver! I refuse to waver, and I will remain in faith — nothing wavering! I'm solid and I know it will all work out as I live and walk by faith."

Hebrews 10:35-36 (KJV), "Cast not away therefore your confidence, which hath

great recompence of reward. For ye have
need of patience, that, after ye have
done the will of God, ye might receive
the promise."
Say this: "I will not throw away my
confidence. I have full confidence that
what God said shall come to pass no
matter what it looks or feels like."

Hebrews 11:11 (KJV), "Through faith also
Sara herself received strength to
conceive seed, and was delivered of a
child when she was past age, because
she judged him faithful who had
promised."

Say this: "God is faithful to keep all His
promises, so I don't have to fear because
God is faithful. He's faithful to keep His
promises."

James 4:7 (KJV), "Submit yourselves
therefore to God. Resist the devil, and he
will flee from you."
Say this: "God, I give my life to You! I
resist all attacks on my life and my family
in Jesus' Name! I resist the devil and all
his little, low-level demons that try to

bring fear and worry into my life. The devil must flee from me! I resist him steadfast with my faith!"

Isaiah 54:17 (NKJV), "'No weapon formed against you shall prosper, And every tongue *which* rises against you in judgment You shall condemn. This *is* the heritage of the servants of the LORD, And their righteousness *is* from Me,' Says the Lord."

Say this: "No weapon formed against me shall prosper, and every tongue that rises against me in judgment is condemned. Fear may form against me, but it will NOT prosper."

1 John 4:18 (NKJV), "There is no fear in love; but perfect love casts out fear, because fear involves torment. But he who fears has not been made perfect in love."

Say this: "God loves me just as much as He loves Jesus. The love of God is shed abroad in my heart by the Holy Spirit and perfect love casts out all fear. Fear and

every bondage, you get out of my mind right now in Jesus' Name. Leave me now in the Name of Jesus!"

John 14:1 (AMP), "Do not let your heart be troubled (afraid, cowardly). Believe [confidently] in God *and* trust in Him, [have faith, hold on to it, rely on it, keep going and] believe also in Me."

Say this: "I don't allow my heart to be troubled because I trust in the Lord. I refuse to allow the enemy to trouble me. I'm at rest and peace and I trust God."

Deuteronomy 31:8 (KJV), "And the LORD, he it is that doth go before thee; he will be with thee, he will not fail thee, neither forsake thee: fear not, neither be dismayed."

Say this: "God will never leave me or forsake me so I refuse to be in fear, and I will not be discouraged because God is with me."

Confessions for the Mind

Isaiah 26:3 (NKJV), "You will keep *him* in perfect peace, *whose* mind *is* stayed *on You,* Because he trusts in You."

Say this: "My mind is at peace, my mind is at rest, my mind is staying on the Lord, and I will not be distracted, in Jesus' Name."

2 Timothy 1:7 (KJV), "For God hath not given us the spirit of fear; but of power, and of love, and of a sound mind."

Say this: "I have a sound mind in Jesus' Name, and I am stable and not going crazy!"

Romans 8:6 (KJV), "For to be carnally minded is death; but to be spiritually minded is life and peace."

Say this: "I am spiritually minded, and I have life and peace."

Ephesians 4:23 (KJV), "and be renewed in the spirit of your mind."

Say this: "I have a renewed mind in the Name of Jesus. I have a new way of thinking, and I will not go back to the old carnal way of thinking."

Philippians 4:6-7 (AMP), "Do not be anxious *or* worried about anything, but in everything [every circumstance and situation] by prayer and petition with thanksgiving, continue to make your [specific] requests known to God. And the peace of God [that peace which reassures the heart, that peace] which transcends all understanding, [that peace which] stands guard over your hearts and your minds in Christ Jesus [is yours]."

Say this: "My mind is guarded by Christ Jesus and I'm not anxious about anything. The peace of God rests in my heart and in my mind. I live in peace, and I will NOT allow anything to steal the peace of God in my life."

Colossians 3:2 (AMP), "Set your mind *and* keep focused *habitually* on the things above [the heavenly things], not on things that are on the earth [which have only temporal value]."

Say this: "My mind is focused and set on things above! I refuse to be distracted!"

1 Peter 1:13 (AMP), "So prepare your minds for action, be completely sober [in spirit—steadfast, self-disciplined, spiritually and morally alert], fix your hope completely on the grace [of God] that is coming to you when Jesus Christ is revealed."

Say this: "I am sober-minded, steadfast, self-disciplined and spiritually and morally alert."

Confusion

1 Corinthians 14:33 (KJV), "For God is not the author of confusion, but of peace, as in all churches of the saints."

Say this: "My mind is not confused in Jesus' Name. I think clearly and have discernment in all areas of my life."

James 1:8 (KJV), "A double minded man is unstable in all his ways."

Say this: "I choose to be single-minded and focused on God's Word. I am not unstable, and I have stability through God's Word."

Depression

Psalm 34:17 (NKJV), "*The righteous* cry out, and the LORD hears, And delivers them out of all their troubles."

Say this: "The Lord hears me, and I am delivered from all my troubles!"

Psalm 42:11 (TLB), "But, O my soul, don't be discouraged. Don't be upset. Expect God to act! For I know that I shall again have plenty of reason to praise him for all that he will do. He is my help! He is my God!"

Say this: "I put all my hope in God in the middle of my troubles, and I praise God for the victory! I refuse to be discouraged and upset. God is my help, and I will never have to worry about God not helping me."

2 Corinthians 1:3-4 (TLB), "What a wonderful God we have—he is the Father of our Lord Jesus Christ, the source of every mercy, and the one who so wonderfully comforts and strengthens us in our hardships and trials. And why does he do this? So that when others are troubled, needing our sympathy and encouragement, we can pass on to them this same help and comfort God has given us."

Say this: "God, thank You for Your comfort in what I'm facing. I refuse to allow the enemy to make me feel abandoned. God comforts me in all my troubles. I receive that comfort! God is my source of all comfort!"

Psalm 40:1-3 (TLB), "I waited patiently for God to help me; then he listened and heard my cry. He lifted me out of the pit of despair, out from the bog and the mire, and set my feet on a hard, firm path, and steadied me as I walked along. He has given me a new song to sing, of praises to our God. Now many will hear of the glorious things he did for me, and stand in awe before the Lord, and put their trust in him."

Say this: "The Lord picks me up and puts me on solid ground. It may feel like shaky times, but I am entering into a new season with a new song in my heart. Thank you, Lord, for bringing me out of the pit of despair!"

Anxiety

Philippians 4:6-7 (AMP), "Do not be anxious *or* worried about anything, but in everything [every circumstance and situation] by prayer and petition with thanksgiving, continue to make your [specific] requests known to God. And the peace of God [that peace which reassures the heart, that peace] which transcends all understanding, [that peace which] stands guard over your hearts and your minds in Christ Jesus [is yours]."

Say this: "I refuse to be anxious, and I receive the peace of God in my life. I will not allow anything to steal my peace no matter what it looks like or feels like. I will not be anxious or worried about anything."

Jeremiah 29:11 (AMP), "'For I know the plans *and* thoughts that I have for you,' says the LORD, 'plans for peace *and* well-being and not for disaster, to give you a future and a hope.'"

Say this: "I have a future and I have hope! God loves me and has a great plan for my life, and I will not give up on that plan."

John 14:27 (TLB), "I am leaving you with a gift—peace of mind and heart! And the peace I give isn't fragile like the peace the world gives. So don't be troubled or afraid."

Say this: "I have the peace of God, so I refuse to worry and allow anxiety to torment me. I'm not worried about anything!"

THE WAR ON WORRY

Is there any reason you can't receive Jesus today?

I believe there is no reason why you can't receive Him into your heart right now. He will give you eternal life, and you can be sure that you will experience the
greater life He has waiting for you. Here is how you receive Him. Just pray this prayer:

Father, I believe that Jesus Christ died on a cross for my sins and I believe that He rose again from the dead. I confess Jesus Christ as my Lord today and thank Him for cleansing me from all unrighteousness. I ask you, Lord, to fill me with Your precious Holy Spirit. I receive it right now! Just as I received Jesus, I receive the baptism of the Holy Spirit right now!

THE WAR ON WORRY

THE WAR ON WORRY